*K*nowledge will forever govern ignorance
... a people who mean to be their own governors
must arm themselves with the power which
knowledge gives.

James Madison

THEN AND NOW
James Madison University

Photographed by Kenneth Garrett

HARMONY HOUSE

PUBLISHERS-LOUISVILLE

Executive Editors: William Butler and William Strode
Library of Congress Catalog Number: 91-70920
Hardcover International Standard Book Number 0-916509-83-4
Printed in The Republic of Korea by Sung In Printing Company, LTD.
through Vivid Color Separation, New York, N.Y.
First Edition printed Spring, 1992 by Harmony House Publishers,
P.O. Box 90, Prospect, Kentucky 40059 (502) 228-2010 / 228-4446
Copyright © 1992 by Harmony House Publishers
Photographs copyright © 1992 by Kenneth Garrett

PREFACE

From the serene beauty of the Quadrangle to the raucous excitement of the Electric Zoo, there is something very special about James Madison University.

There are other outstanding colleges and universities in America. There are other attractive campuses.

But there is only one James Madison University.

The "JMU Way" sets our great University apart from the others. This distinctive method of caring about one another and treating one another with respect and concern gives James Madison University the unique character that makes it so cherished by us all.

These pages contain photographs that do a superb job in reflecting the essence of our great University. They not only capture a lasting image of the way the University exists today, they also provide us with a gateway to the past so we can review the rich heritage that is part of JMU.

It is my hope that this book occupies a place of pride in your home and serves as a means to re-acquaint you with your University and remind you of those very special moments — and those very special people — at James Madison University.

Ronald E. Carrier

Ronald E. Carrier
President

INTRODUCTION

By Fred D. Hilton
Director of Media Services
James Madison University

Since its founding in 1908, James Madison University has evolved into one of the premier public institutions of higher education in America.

JMU has become known as a "Public Ivy" — a public university with the quality of the prestigious private Ivy League colleges.

In recent years, JMU's excellence has been cited in national studies done by *U.S. News and World Report, USA Today, Money* magazine, *Changing Times* magazine, the education editor of *The New York Times* and several books and college guides.

Much of JMU's success is due to its well-deserved reputation for innovation and forward-thinking.

Under the dynamic leadership of Dr. Ronald E. Carrier, who has been president of JMU since 1971, the institution has become a national model in such areas as computer literacy, assessment, global education and the use of technology in the curriculum.

JMU is well-known in higher education for the emphasis it places on effective development of students. Students learn outside, as well as inside, the classroom at JMU.

The learning experience at JMU extends to all parts of campus — from the classroom to the residence halls to dining areas to social and recreational activities.

The University is committed to helping and supporting students, but also to challenging them to achieve their maximum potential.

Superlative teaching is emphasized at JMU and is stressed heavily among the University's outstanding faculty. JMU's acclaimed freshman seminar encourages critical thinking as students are exposed to classic texts.

New approaches to education are continually being explored at the University. Plans are under way to make the University's Carrier Library a model for the nation in the retrieval of information.

JMU's new College of Integrated Science and Technology will open in the mid-1990s and make new avenues of technological expertise available to JMU students.

Students at the University are prepared to take their place in a world which has grown smaller through the tremendous advances that have been made in technology, communications and transportation.

At JMU, students are prepared for the present — but they are also prepared for the 21st Century.

JMU is named for the fourth president of the United States and is the only college or university in America named for President James Madison.

Founded in 1908 as a state normal school, JMU has operated under five different names.

The name James Madison University was first used in 1977 when the institution was awarded university status. JMU has quintupled in size in the last 25 years.

Although the University dates back nearly to the turn of the century, JMU maintains a modern look. Almost half of its 90 major buildings have been constructed since 1970, during the presidency of Dr. Carrier.

JMU is located in the heart of Virginia's famous Shenandoah Valley. The University's beautifully-landscaped campus contains 472 acres — including a large lake — and borders Interstate 81.

There are more than 11,000 students at JMU, with the number of men and women students about equal.

JMU is extremely popular among prospective students. Only one of each seven applicants can be enrolled.

Nearly 80 percent of the JMU students are Virginians. The others come from throughout the United States and many foreign countries.

More than 100 different degree programs on the bachelor's, master's and educational specialist level are offered at JMU.

There are a wide range of courses available in the College of Letters and Sciences, the College of Business, the College of Education and Psychology, the College of Fine Arts and Communication, the College of Health and Human Services, and the Graduate School.

JMU has an extensive and highly successful program of intercollegiate athletics. Teams compete in Division I of the NCAA.

The University was established by the Virginia General Assembly in 1908 as the State Normal and Industrial School for Women at Harrisonburg.

The first president of the University was Julian Ashby Burruss. The University opened its doors in the fall of 1909 with an enrollment of 150 students and a faculty of 15. The first 20 graduates received diplomas in 1911.

In 1914, the name of the University was shortened to the State Normal School for Women at Harrisonburg. Authorization to award bachelor's degrees was granted in 1916.

During this initial period of the University's development, the campus plan was established and six buildings were constructed.

Dr. Samuel Page Duke became the second president of the University in 1919 upon the resignation of Mr. Burruss, who became president of Virginia Tech.

The University became the State Teachers College at Harrisonburg in 1924 and continued under that name until 1938 when it was named Madison College in honor of James Madison.

During Dr. Duke's administration, nine major buildings were constructed and, in 1946, men were first enrolled as regular day students.

In 1949, following Dr. Duke's retirement, Dr. G. Tyler Miller became the third president of the University.

During Dr. Miller's administration, from 1949 to 1970, the campus was enlarged by 240 acres and 19 buildings were constructed. Major curriculum changes were made and the University was authorized to award master's degrees in 1954.

In 1966, by action of the Virginia General Assembly, the University constructed men's residence halls and became fully co-educational.

Dr. Ronald E. Carrier became the University's fourth president in 1971. During his administration, the institution has grown significantly and reached its current position of national prominence.

A SELECTED JMU CHRONOLOGY

1908 On March 14, Virginia Governor Claude A. Swanson signed the General Assembly bill creating the State Normal and Industrial School for Women at Harrisonburg; Julian Ashby Burruss was named president of the new school.

1909 The school opened with an enrollment of 150 and a faculty of 15.

1910 The school operated its first summer session (the first ever held in Virginia). Men and women students attended.

1911 The first 20 graduates received diplomas.

1914 The school's name was shortened to the State Normal School for Women at Harrisonburg.

1916 Authorization was received for the school to award bachelor's degrees. Previously, only diplomas for post-high school work had been awarded.

1919 Dr. Samuel Page Duke became the institution's second president.

1924 The institution was renamed the State Teachers College at Harrisonburg.

1938 The institution was renamed Madison College in honor of President James Madison; Enrollment passed 1,000.

1946 Men enrolled as day students for the first time during the institution's regular session.

1949 Dr. G. Tyler Miller became the institution's third president.

1954 The college was authorized to award master's degrees.

1964 Enrollment passed 2,000.

1966 The General Assembly approved full coeducational status for the college, and men were enrolled as resident students for the first time.

1971 Dr. Ronald E. Carrier became the institution's fourth president; Academic divisions were reorganized into schools which eventually became the College of Letters and Sciences; the College of Business; the College of Education and Psychology; the College of Fine Arts and Communication; the College of Health and Human Services; and the Graduate School.

1972 Enrollment passed 5,000.

1977 The institution was renamed James Madison University.

1979 The university was authorized to award educational specialist degrees.

1983 JMU celebrated its 75th anniversary; The first honorary doctoral degrees were awarded.

1987 Enrollment passed 10,000.

1989 Planning began for the establishment of a new College of Integrated Science and Technology.

1990 Enrollment passed 11,000.

It will be the first time since Jefferson founded the University of Virginia that a great school has been organized on strictly definite, scientific, pedagogical principles before a nail is driven or a class taught. It presents the ideals for a really great school — one worthy of the Valley of Virginia — that can be completed in ten years or less, without wasting a dime or an ounce of effort. When completed, it will be beyond comparison. The most beautiful, the most comprehensive school of its kind in the South — and indeed will have few equals anywhere.

State Superintendent of Public Instruction
Joseph D. Eggleston, 1908

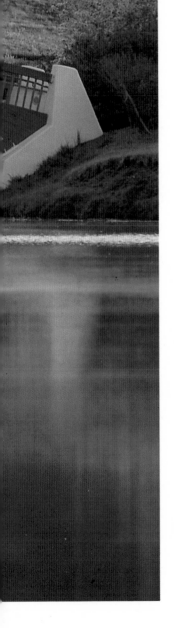

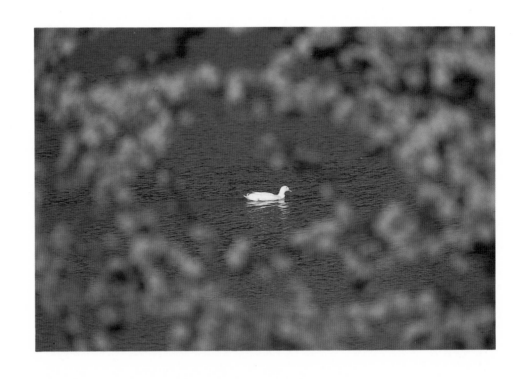

The Early Years

Looking across campus

*The diffusion of knowledge is the
only guardian of liberty.*

James Madison

Print depicting an aerial view of campus

Blue Stone Hill shortly after the completion of dormitory number 2

Reed Hall

View from Hillcrest, 1925

The Rock

Ground is broken in May of 1914 for the Student building (now Harrison Hall)

A dormitory room at the Normal

Spotswood Hall, 1925

Hillcrest, 1925

Foundation work begins on Wilson Hall, 1930

The laying of Wilson Hall's cornerstone, 1930

Wilson Hall, 1933

The new Madison Memorial Library lobby and Joan of Arc, about 1939

44

Cleveland Cottage

Aerial view of campus, 1937

Senior Hall, 1948

Madison Memorial Library, 1948

JMU TODAY

James Madison University

Learned institutions ought to be the favorite objects with every free people. They throw that light over the public mind which is the best security against crafty and dangerous encroachments on the public liberty.

James Madison

48

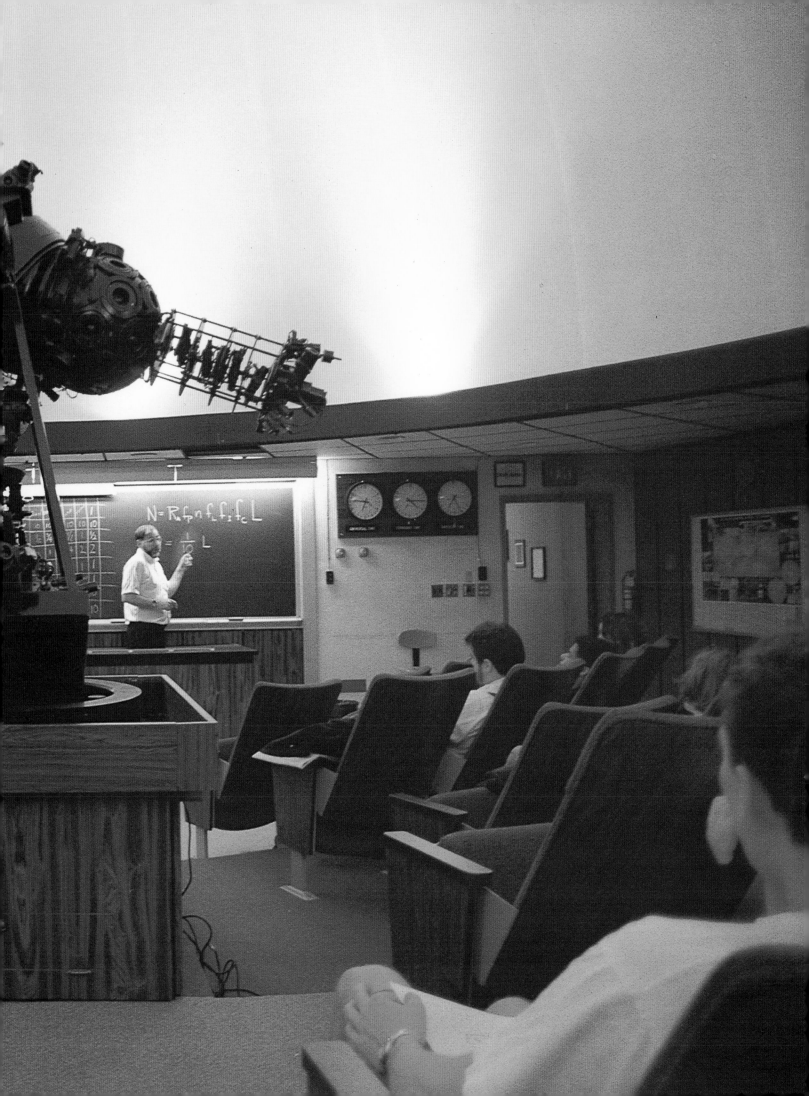

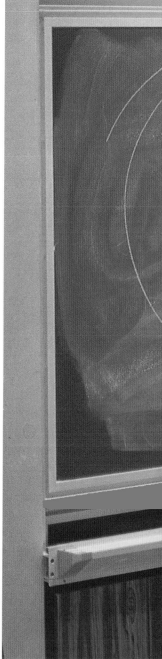

55

James Madison University is committed to . . . a broad liberal arts program for all students and the integration of the liberal arts into the student's major.

Mission Statement, James Madison University

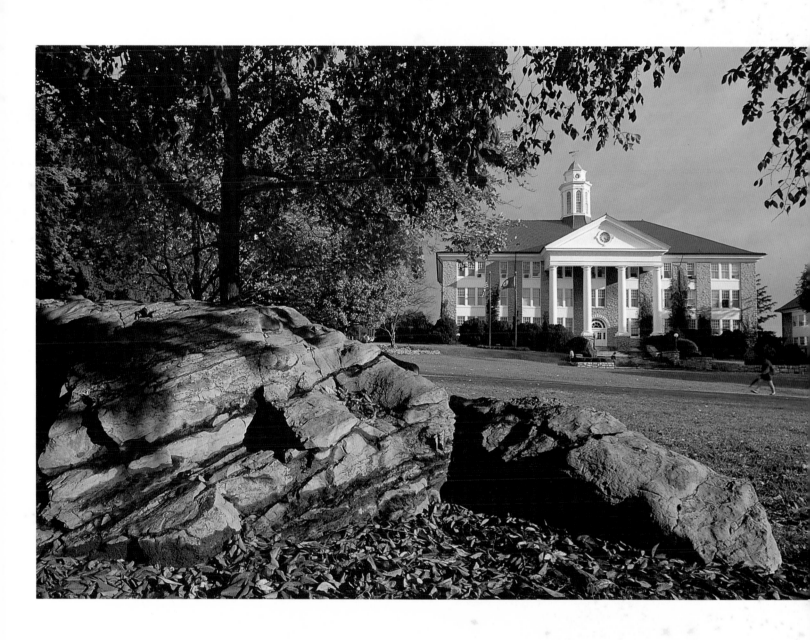

Catching the train at the C. & W. junction near campus

A cooking class in Science Hall during the first decade

The faculty in academic costume for the first time for the groundbreaking for Spotswood Hall

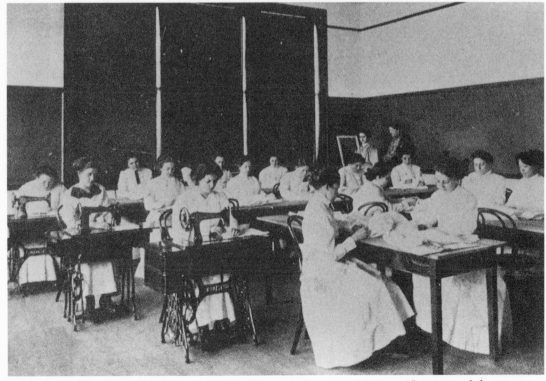

The sewing laboratory,

The Glee Club, 1913

A student assembly

Executive Board of Student Activities, 1917

Reed gym as combination gymnasium and auditorium

The Glee Club poses on the quad in 1922

The Normal's second auditorium— the western end of Harrison Dining Hall

Chapel exercises, 1933

Classroom, 1939

Horseback riding, 1944

Archery club, 1948

THE JMU WAY

James Madison University

hat spectacle can be more edifying or
more seasonable, than that of liberty and
learning, each leaning on the other for
their mutual and surest support?

James Madison

...the men who coach and play basketball at James Madison University love it. Conversely, the men who coach at Virginia's other eight Division I schools hate it. So much that they have voted JMU's year-old Convocation Center as the most unfriendly arena in the Old Dominion.

Richmond News-Leader, December 14, 1983

Thousands of men and women who studied at Madison . . . took with them sound academic and professional preparation. They were also imbued with a spirit of friendship, a respect for honor, a desire for service and a realization of the importance of values. These principles had been imbued in the spirit of the school.

Raymond C. Dingledine, in *Madison College: The First Fifty Years*

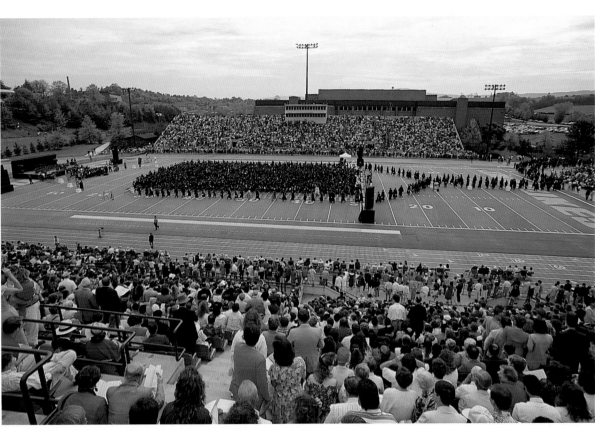

The Apache Hockey team of 1914

Junior basketball team , 1912

The participants in the first tennis tournament at the Normal

May Day, 1927

Cotillion dance, 1933

May Day activities, 1937

The May Queen and her Maid of Honor, 1939

Formal dance, 1939

In a dorm room in the early 1940s

May Day exercises in front of Converse Hall, 1950

Dancing in Reed gymnasium — formal dresses but no men

When football came to James Madison, it was soon followed by the Hillside Gang

Home Economics majors present the faculty to the freshman with an opening tea, 1956